THE IMMERSION METHOD

How to Learn Any Language to
Fluency the Fun and Easy Way

4th Edition

ERIC BODNAR

ISBN: 9781793103307

TABLE OF CONTENTS

PART ONE

The Method

LANGUAGE LEARNING HELL

It's hard to argue against the value of hard work. It creates high-quality results. It pushes people to do what they need to do. It gets things done. But in the case of learning a foreign language, hard work can be misleading.

Language learning is unique in that way. It's a skill built upon learning and memorizing thousands of words, phrases, and grammar structures. Reading and understanding this information can be quite difficult, and then, native speakers spit all of this out at seemingly a bazillion words a minute. Many decide to take on this challenge enthusiastically with hard work and ultra-high determination, and I did the same a number of years ago.

Korean was my first foreign language that I attempted to self-study. After only a month of learning just a few basic phrases and somewhere around 100 words from my textbook, I relocated to South Korea to work as an English teacher by day and study by night. It was my first time being outside of my home country, and I was surrounded by a new language that I was hungry to learn. For the four years I lived there, there was a determination inside of me that burned red-hot.

It took four years before I realized that something was seriously wrong. At that point, I was confident that I was fast approaching fluency based upon my growing conversational ability and frequent reading of native-level materials like news articles and short stories. Underneath it all, however, was deep dissatisfaction. I wasn't happy at all with the life that I had created.

I chose a life of study and learning, but it eventually developed into a painful and agonizing routine for the sake of more and more progress. This routine was the most effective way to learn that I knew at the time. It helped me to remember more words than any other technique I had used in the past four years.

A major component of that routine was these super difficult flashcards that I created. The front side provided a lengthy sentence or two in English, and I gave myself the task to recall it in Korean near verbatim as written on the backside. They got me to think in Korean and actively recall new vocabulary in the context of sentences. They were also immensely stressful. Stress can be a good thing but not so much for the kind that threatens your mental well-being.

When I would guess incorrectly, I would get legitimately angry at myself. I remember thinking, "I would be fluent by now if only I had the same memory abilities like those famous polyglots. How can these people learn four or more languages when I struggle so much with just one?" I figured that if seemingly superhuman people like renowned polyglot Alexander Arguelles can study eight hours a day, so can I."

I would honor my commitment to learning fluent Korean by spending Saturday mornings and afternoons dissecting entire short stories and newspaper articles line by line. Sundays were dedicated to my three hour grammar book sessions at my favorite cafes in Seoul. If I wasn't making more tortuous flashcards from new sentences, I copied them down in my notebook in full and recited them multiple times painstakingly. At night, I *rewarded* myself by watching Korean talk shows which did little to keep me interested but was *good* for learning conversational Korean.

I was desperate for change. I had created my own personal language learning hell. It took a close friend to help convince me to start a new life in a new country. I decided to move to Japan and start learning Japanese. Before leaving Korea, I had told one of my Korean mentors about my decision, too. He warned me that I would have to start all the way back from zero as if I was about to lose four years of hard work.

It was one of those rare occasions where I ignored all logic and reasoning and listened to my heart and intuition. It felt so peaceful and zen-like to let go of the baggage that I worked so hard to collect and just follow what seemed to be destiny. I felt free starting over on a blank slate and drawn towards new paths to find more exciting and fun ways to learn languages.

Starting From Zero Again

If plenty of linguists and polyglots have mastered multiple languages by themselves without schooling, there was still hope I could get it right. As I tried a completely different path based on putting enjoyment first, I realized I was starting to once again enjoy the mystical and spellbinding process of learning a foreign language.

For seven years, I read up on hundreds of learning methods and experimented on myself with Korean and Japanese. This includes Scriptorium, Shadowing, audio-based lessons, immersion, language exchanges, flashcards, Anki, online courses, language learning software, memory techniques, extensive reading, news articles, and textbooks. I took the few bits and pieces that were effective in each routine, combined them, and tweaked with them day and night until everything clicked at last.

I had found the routine that I was seeking to quickly memorize thousands of vocabulary words, phrases, and grammar points with very little stress involved, and it could easily be applied to any foreign language. I enjoy it so much that I felt compelled to write this book to share that method with others who might be looking for more fun and effective learning routines. If the study methods mentioned earlier sound painfully similar to what you have been doing to learn foreign languages, I assure you that there is another way.

Fortunately for you, there is no need to undergo eight hour study routines daily and use medieval-like learning methods as I did in the past. A solid 45-90 minutes of intensive reading and learning followed by a habit of freely reading, listening to, and watching foreign material for pleasure is much easier to maintain in the long-term. With all the vocabulary and complex grammatical rules, it's easy to think of language learning as a test of willpower and determination, but that's not true when you use smart language learning methods and make it fun each and every day.

Why People Fail in Learning a Language

Many dedicated language learners like myself burnout after trying so hard to learn, but the term "burnout" does not quite capture this problem in full. The real issue preventing many people from learning a foreign language is their definition of what it means to learn languages. That problematic definition is formed from being required to take unimaginative and uninspired Spanish and French classes in high school and college. That definition is what causes burnout.

In the beginner phase or at any level, it would be a huge mistake to exclude content made by native speakers for native speakers in the target language. Beginners to language learning often omit this content in favor of more learning from traditional materials like textbooks, online courses, and educational podcasts. I have made that mistake not once or twice but continuously for several years with Korean. Even when I did choose to include them, it was always boring things that were *good* sources to learn conversational Korean from. I forced myself again and again to try to like popular talk shows and variety shows.

There were many things I loved to do in the language, but I didn't understand how to effectively learn from these materials. For example, I loved to play video games in Korean. But do you stop playing to look up each new word that you find? When do you actually just play the game? The hardcore learner that I was tried to learn every new word, and that never lasted past 10 minutes. And when I did let myself play the game, it felt like I wasn't learning anything.

My number one goal for four years was to learn fluent Korean above all else, so progress at any cost was the mindset. It was my vision for my future and a part of my identity. Sure, I had eventually reached a certain degree of conversational fluency but at what cost? Progress blinded me to the fact that my internal fun and motivation meter was gradually sinking and eventually hovering just above zero. And then, it hit zero.

It hit zero multiple times while living in South Korea, a country where I was immersed in the language. Several days would pass without me wanting to doing anything with Korean, and I blamed my laziness and lack of discipline. In hindsight, I can now say that there were two much more important factors that led to these difficult times of zero growth and even regression.

The first is my language learning methods were poor and perhaps even a little masochistic. The second is my idea of having fun with Korean was to watch Korean TV that I disliked deep inside, yet I forced myself to watch for the sake of learning. I used to think that I disliked it because I didn't understand enough. I thought that once I was able to understand most of it I would eventually come to like it. Now, that may or may not be true, but there were materials that I was clearly more interested in. And I neglected them.

I gave up too easily trying to learn from the things I truly cared about. I questioned their usefulness in everyday conversation. Why would I ever need to know "flaming hydra" and "disintegration beam" from Korean video games when I should be learning practical things like "plant a tree" and "brew coffee"? I repeatedly put off fun materials in favor of more practical ones.

But the truth is that you can learn all of that and learn it easily. This book will show you how to balance all of this learning and retain it effectively. You can learn primarily from what you love and use it to learn practical vocabulary as you go along. Love is what makes all of this learning possible. Without love, learning is meaningless.

So, What's the Method?

Immerse yourself in any kind of foreign material that you love without any English subtitles or translations for roughly 20 minutes or so. This can include reading up on topics that you are highly interested in, watching exciting foreign shows and movies, listening to your favorite music, or even playing video games in foreign languages. For this brief amount of time, very carefully listen and look for words unknown to you and that are repeated multiple times. Without stopping the reading, video, or audio, quickly jot down the unknown words that are repeated two or more times and continue without looking anything up in the dictionary. Include the page numbers, video times, audio track times, or in-game screenshots for reference later.

After the 20 minutes or so have passed, stop and review your jotted notes, and pick the two lines or words that you are the most curious to learn. This will be easier to do with written materials, and some effort may be required to find video materials with transcriptions and subtitles in the target language. Next, use online dictionaries and grammar resources to quickly break down the lines to learn their meaning. After fully learning these lines, create very specific reading, writing, listening, and speaking practice exercises a free program called Anki (www.ankisrs.net). These exercises will help you practice both the lines you select and the more practical example sentences you find in online dictionaries and grammar resources.

As you consistently mine a particular topic, genre, or series and regularly do these exercises, you will come to understand more of it very fast. You'll be actively searching for the high frequency words and learning them. These words are the key to slowly understanding what everyone is saying and what the main idea is. The Anki exercises are just as important in not forgetting those key words. This includes being able to recognize them by eye and ear and produce them when writing or speaking.

If you are in the beginning stages of learning your target language, this technique is highly recommended as you progress through learning the basics. Reading, breaking down, and learning from native-level materials like TV, novels, and videos will be difficult at first, but early attempts to learn from these materials will immediately connect you to the real language used by native speakers every day. This connection will be sure to bring you excitement. It will also help build an early habit of freely reading, listening to, and watching native-level materials without English.

Learning from the real language has the power to spice up your average language learning routine which is often heavily based on traditional language learning materials like textbooks and phrasebooks. Many language learners never make it past the first book and give up when things become too dry and boring, so this method and the other information contained in this book aim to prevent that from happening. A later chapter will cover how to incorporate this method as you learn the basics of your target language.

When you combine learning from native-level materials, learning from traditional language learning materials, creating and doing smart Anki exercises, and interacting with native speakers in your free time every day, you will have the foundation for an effective learning routine.

How to go about combining these activities will be discussed throughout the pages of this book. The method of this book aims to keep you interested and continually learning until you have reached a level that you are personally satisfied with. Going full immersion and doing everything possible in the target language is a very powerful technique to learn, but it is not required. Instead, this book will encourage the habit of consuming foreign materials more and more frequently.

Part I will continue with an explanation about the Anki exercises and how to create them for any foreign language. Part II will provide a beginner's guide to starting a foreign language including advice on how to incorporate some immersion during this early phase. If you are not a beginner, you may still find a few helpful techniques here to add to your learning routine. Part III will cover how to create your own individualized learning program from the foreign material that you love.

SMARTER WAYS TO LEARN

In general, rereading and re-listening in mass to new language that you wish to learn is not very efficient in helping you retain that new information. You may also find it tedious and boring. Anki aims to improve your memory of new information by testing your ability to actively recall it through intelligent flashcard exercises.

I don't like to say the method of this book is flashcards because we were all taught to use boring, primitive flashcards in our school days. I speak of the ones where the front side would read "this animal has eyes bigger than its brain" and the back would read "ostrich." They were dry and dull, and they remind us of the useless facts that we were required to memorize for school tests and forgot just a week later.

In this book, we will look at Production, Cloze, Listening, and Shadowing exercises. Two rules govern these exercises. First, choose easy. Second, choose fun.

These rules act as daily reminders to prevent the burnout that causes many language learners to quit temporarily or indefinitely. These four exercise types will help you to fully understand any new words, phrases, or grammar that you wish to learn and master. They will train you in all five of the language skills: reading, writing, speaking, listening, and thinking.

This chapter is dedicated to describing the purpose of each exercise, and the rationale behind why specifically these exercises were chosen. A set of examples, images, and how to instructions will be provided in the next chapter.

Production

Let us begin with the basic flashcard exercise that you are probably already familiar with. You might have made a few of these if you have ever used flashcards or Anki to help you learn a new language. Simply, you'll be given a word or picture in English and have to say the equivalent word aloud in the target language. That's it.

For many years I held a strong and bitter dislike for these kinds of flashcards, and I imagine many others out there hold similar feelings. They get really boring really fast. They can give us the feeling that we are back in school cramming for our next test. I abandoned these cards after having much more success with Cloze, Listening, and Shadowing exercises, so why would I ever go back to these stupid things? In recent years, however, I realized that they do have a use.

The problem arises when you do nothing but this exercise in Anki. When you have a strong mix and balance of other exercises to go with this simple one, this exercise is perfect. Our ability to speak a new language is greatly enhanced just by being able to recall thousands of vocabulary and phrases with lightning speed and little to no trouble. We need to know how to quickly say things like red, square, professor, power cable, dehydration, open the door, turn the lights off, and throw a ball. That's where Production exercises in the right quantity can help us.

In these Production exercises, we can test not only our ability to recall vocabulary and phrases but to say these words with correct pronunciation and with a reduced accent. Take this time to pay great attention to how you pronounce words. Apply what you have learned in studying the phonetics of your target language.

What if we reverse the order and put the target language on the front and English on the back? This would change the Production exercise to a reading and translation exercise, which is useful, yet we will get plenty of reading from our Cloze and Shadowing exercises as well as through the textbook. Additionally, the Listening exercises will give us a more interesting way to test our recognition of these words.

Putting just the English word on the front side of this flashcard saves a lot of time, and you could also put an image representing the word here in an effort to use as little English as possible. The choice is yours. Abstract words like "nonsense" and "discipline" will be much more difficult to find proper images for, so the English word might be the easiest option. If you are looking to use as little English as possible in Anki, Cloze exercises offer an alternative way to test our recall ability for these abstract words.

Stick with just single words and small phrases. If we put English sentences on the front and try to recall them in full in the target language as mentioned last chapter, we can potentially put ourselves through language learning hell. The possibility of all kinds of synonyms and different translations makes it frustrating. Too many questions come up when we think of answers in our minds that seem correct yet are different from the answer on the back. You might find yourself irritated wondering whether or not the answer that you came up with is correct or not. It's tedious and not a very pleasant learning experience.

Let's say we want to learn from a basic sentence like "**冷蔵庫のドアを開いたらリンゴが落ちた**" which means "when I opened the door of the refrigerator, the apple fell out." Instead of trying to memorize the full sentence, use these basic Production exercises to help you memorize single words like **冷蔵庫**(refrigerator), **ドア** (door), **開く** (to open), **りんご** (apple), and **落ちた** (fell). Make exercises for very short phrases like **冷蔵庫のドア** (refrigerator door) and **リンゴが落ちた**

(the apple fell).

Cloze

In Cloze, we are using context to figure out what one word and one word only is missing from a sentence or two or even a large context that we have learned beforehand. Then, we write that one missing word in our notebooks. The game is to select sentences or passages with enough context so that you can easily guess what is missing. Let's take a few sentences from the last chapter as a quick example in English:

"You'll be actively searching for the high frequency words and learning them. These words are the key to slowly understanding what everyone is saying and what the main [...] is."

I hope the answer is somewhat obvious. We can essentially do this in our target language to practice vocabulary in context, grammar particles, and verb conjugations. Even set phrases can be learned one word at a time within large contexts. It may look silly and simple like an elementary school exercise, but that is precisely the point to learning elementary phrases, grammar, and conjugations.

Reading, thinking, and writing in the target language are all involved. Many of us dream to be able to think in foreign languages, so here is a start. Here we are reading and thinking in the foreign language while actively trying to find the one missing word. We then write the answer in that language in our notebooks. There is no need to write the same word down repeatedly or copy sentences in full. It's just one word written one time.

If you are in a place where paper and pencil is inconvenient like as a bus or train, simply write the answer in the palm of your hand to make this exercise doable on the go. Rather than focusing on whether or not other people think you are some kind of palm reader, let us focus on the fact that we can transform travel time into learning time.

Foreign Writing Systems

If you are a beginner and would like to try these Cloze exercises, you will need to learn that language's writing system as quickly as you can. Western languages like English, German, Spanish, French, or Italian share the Latin-Roman alphabet, which makes this process relatively easier. For those learning languages that do not use this alphabet like Arabic, Thai, Japanese, Korean, and Chinese, there is still no need to worry.

Plenty of great supplementary books and free online resources exist to make writing manageable step by step. On the easy side of the spectrum, Korean's brilliant Hangul system takes just a mere few weeks to become comfortable within it. Others may extend into the months and some into years like Chinese and Japanese. For these languages, your writing pace will be a bit slow in the beginning, and there is likely to be some confusion. Yet, it is important to take early action towards strong foreign literacy skills.

It is highly recommended to **NOT** write in romanized versions for these non-Western languages, as this creates a huge self-imposed barrier to reading and writing in your target language. That barrier becomes increasingly harder to remove as habits form in the early days of your language learning journey. If you choose to write in romaji for your Japanese Cloze cards for example, you will be blocking a huge opportunity to immerse yourself in the written language.

I remember thinking how stupid my Korean textbook was for not including the Romanized readings for every word and sentence. I ended up scribbling in a butchered Romanized version over the majority of the sentences from the book. Unknown to me and my stupidity, my book was trying to teach me fundamental lessons that I completely ignored. By ignoring the written system, I was creating that self-imposed barrier to reading and writing and even the basics of Korean pronunciation which is rooted in their writing system!

Writing the answers to Cloze exercises can be tedious and slow at first, but your writing speed will increase rapidly within the first month. You'll get used to it. If you can't remember how to write certain non-Latin and non-Roman letters during a Cloze exercise, the other words in the context will often contain the letters needed to write the missing word.

We can even learn to write the complex Chinese hanzi and Japanese kanji characters from memory with the right tools. A strong system of silly and fun mnemonics was the key to helping me learn how to write hundreds of kanji from memory alone. It would be wise to immediately seek high quality books and resources to learn these characters.

Listening

The Listening exercises are simply listening more or less, but Text-to-Speech services completely change how we can practice foreign listening comprehension these days. There exists a way to take words, phrases, and sentences from any source at all and generate free audio recordings of an automated native speaker saying those words. These audio recordings can then be placed inside of Anki to make listening the easiest and most fun language skill to practice. Amazing nor astounding does not even begin to describe this awesome power now available to everybody.

After hearing a two to three second audio file played on the front of these flashcard exercises, it is our task to either think or say aloud the equivalent in our native tongue. We can test our comprehension of single words or sentences in full here. After the file is played, it's either you get it or don't within three seconds. It's a very simple and effective exercise in training our valuable ears to instantly decode meaning of spoken words just like we can in our first language. The Cloze exercises do take a little time and effort to figure out, but the Listening and Production cards help break up the monotony with on the spot lightning round challenges.

On the back side of these flashcard exercises, I recommend putting the English translation and the transcription of the audio file to check for complete comprehension. Cloze and Shadowing will be only in the target language, but using English here is perhaps the simplest way to check if we fully understand the meaning behind the words. Freely listening and watching foreign material without English will be encouraged throughout this book, yet this will be one of the rare cases where it may be more effective to use our native language.

Unlike the Production cards, however, we can test our comprehension of sentences in full one by one. Undoubtedly, there are going to be some synonyms when translating full sentences from one language to another, but it takes much less effort to translate sentences from the target language to our native language. Try it yourself and see how fast they go by.

Shadowing

This last exercise will put the foreign language on our tongues. Shadowing is as simple as playing a sound file of a native speaker and reading and speaking aloud with the audio as best as we can. Two or three times will be enough. It's quite the mouth workout at first, and it remains a good workout to build our vocal muscles as we encounter more language to mimic. It's also challenging and incredibly fun. If you are interested in things like pronunciation, clarity of speech, accent reduction, and reading at native level speeds, this is the exercise for you.

This technique was developed and popularized by professor Alexander Arguelles, and in its original form, it requires long passages and dialogues as well as adequate space to march back and forth in. I would like to include a very shortened form of Shadowing in this program where we just need to read our selected passages along with a native speaker. It would be a wonderful use of your time to learn more about the full technique with a quick internet search.

The original exercise is done by reading aloud in a commanding voice to build speaking confidence and pronounce all the words clearly and correctly, so a home office environment would be ideal. This won't be possible if you are practicing on the bus or train, but if these times are best for you to do these exercises, silently mouthing along or quietly speaking into your hand is better than saying nothing at all.

Unfortunately, this exercise can only be done with video and audio sources, so lines and passages from written materials will sadly be left out. There are methods to get native speakers to record such lines, but they are highly inconvenient and are generally not worth the time and money to acquire them. Also, text to speech robots are not accurate enough yet to imitate proper accent and intonation, so I do not recommend Shadowing after them.

I will admit that this last exercise requires a few hoops to jump through to setup inside of Anki, so if it is too complicated for you, you can practice Shadowing without it. I am in love with the idea of practicing a little of everything inside Anki, but I understand that you may not be willing to acquire video files and extract audio from them. How to do this will be explained in a later chapter.

THE LEARNING MACHINE

Anki will allow us to create all of these flashcard exercises, and it also doubles as a Spaced Repetition System (SRS). The SRS aims to test us on information at intervals just before we are likely to forget. This means easy exercises can be pushed back months and months away until the next time we are tested on them. Difficult exercises will be shown more frequently until we master them. If exercises are too difficult, we can change them to make them winnable again.

We have absolute freedom over what we want to focus on and practice, but this freedom comes at a price. We will have to make our own personal decks based on the materials that we use and what we personally need. We must also stick to a schedule of regularly doing these exercises at a certain point in the day but more on this in the final chapter.

How to Setup

When you download, install, and open up Anki, click 'Create Deck' and name it whatever you like. We will only need one deck for now, as all four of our flashcards will go into this deck. Click 'Add' at the top, and then 'Basic' at the top of the new window. By default, you should see four card types.

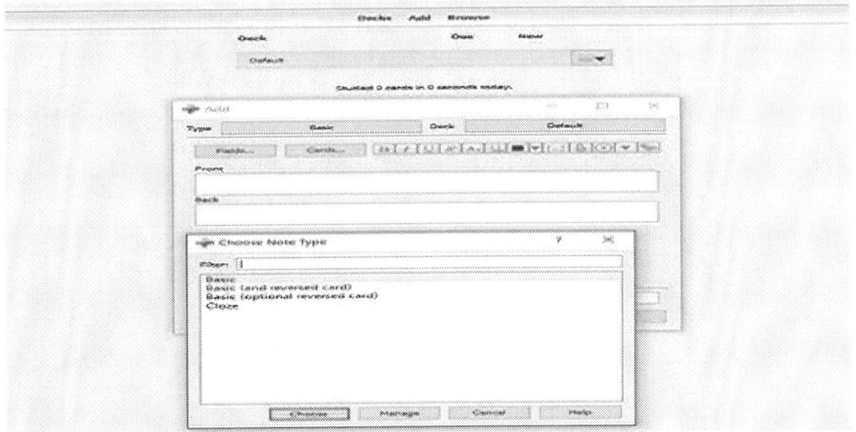

THE ORIGINAL FOUR CARD TYPES IN ANKI

Let's add Production, Listening, and Shadowing cards. Creating card types for each one takes seconds and allows for easy reference and organization if we ever wish to change something in bulk. If you click "Manage", you can delete the unnecessary cards and keep "Cloze". Click "Add" and select "Add:Basic" and rename it to "Production". Repeat this process for "Listening" and "Shadowing."

Next, you will need an add-on called "AwesomeTTS". It's a free Text to Speech service that we can integrate into Anki. This will allow us to do the Listening card types as well as add an extra audio reinforcement to our Production and Cloze cards. With a simple install and Anki reboot, we can simply paste the word or sentence into the 'Front' or 'Back' box, highlight it, and click the speaker icon from the add-on to quickly generate the audio in seconds. In case, AwesomeTTS is ever removed for any reason, the internet provides multiple free Text to Speech services. Let us take this time to be grateful for this technology and how it makes life a little bit easier.

AwesomeTTS: https://ankiweb.net/shared/info/301952613

To demonstrate how to use these exercises, let's use this basic Japanese sentence.

さちこのいえはおおきいいえです。

"Sachiko's house is a big house."

Here's just one way you could create exercises for this sentence. If we don't know the words **いえ** (house) and **おおきい** (big), we should create two Production cards. Simply, put the English word or a picture on the front side, and put the word in the target language on the back side. To add sound to these cards, put the word in the target language twice on the back side. Then, highlight the bottom one, click on the AwesomeTTS icon on the icon bar, and generate an audio clip using the automated speaker of your choice.

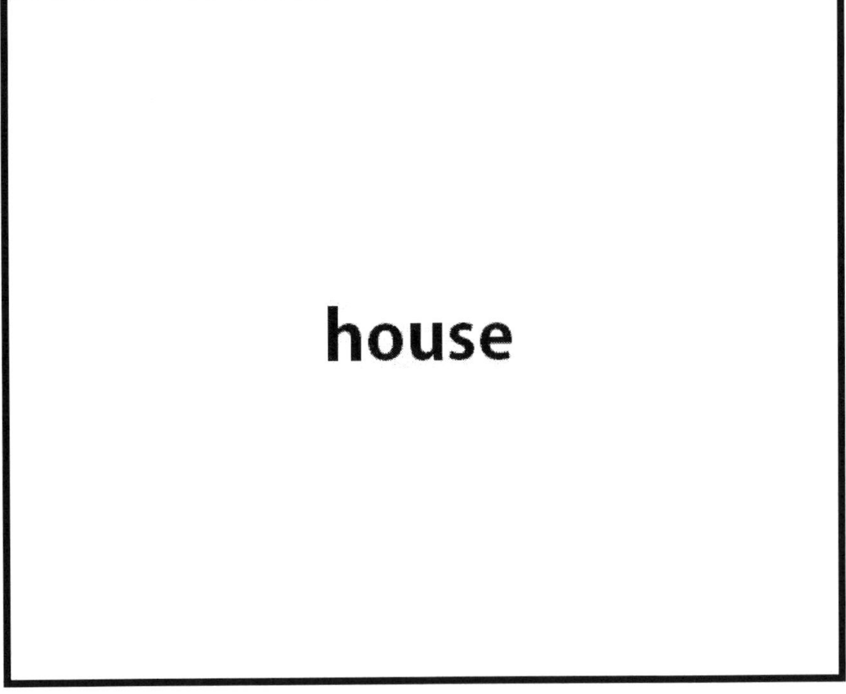

HOW PRODUCTION CARDS APPEAR DURING PRACTICE

Let's switch to Cloze cards. To switch card types, if we are looking at a new blank card after creating your Production cards, click "Type" and select "Cloze".

For Cloze cards, I would not recommend testing the simple vocabulary in this sentence, as it would create too many problems. For example, if we remove いえ (house) from this sentence once, one will still be remaining, and we could simply copy that down into our notebook. We won't be testing our ability to recall or write the word. If we remove both, almost any other word could take it's place! We could write, "Sachiko's elephant is a big elephant", yet the original plan was to test our ability to recall and write house.

Instead, Cloze would be perfect here for testing correct usage of grammar particles. Let's create one for の (a possessive particle) and one for は (a topic marker). To do so, copy and paste the sentence to the front and back. Then, highlight the grammar particle that you wish to practice in the "Text" box. Click the [...] icon. Highlight the sentence on the back of the card or the "Extra" box and create a text to speech file.

さちこ[...]いえはおおきいいえです。

HOW CLOZE CARDS APPEAR DURING PRACTICE

For Listening exercises, let's make two for our two new vocabulary words and an additional one for the entire sentence. Copy and paste the text in your target language in the "Front" box, and then create the AwesomeTTS audio file. Alternatively, you can insert the audio file from your textbook if you plan on Shadowing it inside of Anki. In the “Back” box, put the text in both the target language and your native language.

さちこのいえはおおきいいえです。

(Audio file)

HOW LISTENING CARDS APPEAR DURING PRACTICE

Yes, it will appear blank. When these cards show up during reviews, we will immediately hear the sound file play. In case we need the file to play again, simply press “R” on your keyboard.

Shadowing comes last. As always, remember to switch to the correct card type. Copy and paste the target sentence into the "Front" text box. Press "Enter" twice. Insert your audio clip. Nothing needs to go into the "Back" text box.

さちこのいえはおおきいいえです。

(Text + Audio)

HOW SHADOWING CARDS APPEAR DURING PRACTICE

PART TWO

Getting Started

ONE AND ONLY ONE TEXTBOOK

Early attempts to learn from native-level materials like TV dramas or movies is definitely encouraged for beginners, but without learning the basics of the target language as you progress, your ability will be very limited. You're likely to have some trouble reading and writing the language. Without knowing basic phrases or sentence structures, you'll have a lot of trouble communicating with native speakers. A bad accent can make it very difficult for native speakers to understand you.

There are so many ways to begin learning a foreign language these days, and I don't wish to dictate an exact process of how you should get started. That should be your choice. Start wherever you are drawn to the most! Part II will be a collection of advice and techniques that you may find useful at any level, and it will attempt to offer a guide to those who have little idea on where to start.

You will have more success the more you focus on the things that truly interest you about a foreign language. A few people will study phonetics first for months and years focusing on sounding as native-like as possible. In the case of James Heisig, he decided to first tackle the problem of remembering the meaning and how to write the 2,200+ Japanese kanji characters before learning anything else. He would go on to create one of the most popular programs to teach the Japanese kanji to foreigners.

In general, if you are starting a language from scratch, it would be wise to take the first days, weeks, or more to learn as much as you can about the writing and phonetics systems of the foreign language. Seek multiple sources for information to soak up as much as you can before you begin learning vocabulary and grammar. Studying even basic phonetics can make your speech so much more natural and easier to understand and follow for natives. It may seem silly to start learning a foreign language by learning how to write it, but writing it will allow us to do these Cloze exercises and build a habit of thinking in the target language as well as strong vocabulary, reading, and writing skills.

In the age of technology, quick internet searches, and YouTube, it is possible to learn anything without even a single textbook including a foreign language. For the sake of streamlined learning, I will recommend a coursebook or textbook but a maximum of just one. A high-quality coursebook does provide well-rounded introductions to foreign languages, solid grammar explanations, and a wealth of words, phrases, and sentences to create Anki exercises with.

Coursebooks and other language learning resources provide a safe and sheltered source for learning, yet it is important to escape this language learning bubble as early as possible. Outside of that is where the true language and culture lie. There may be a set of six textbooks to learn Dutch, but you may only need the first one before you are able to learn primarily from material made for native speakers. Smart Anki use and a habit of immersing yourself in native-level materials frequently can make that happen easily.

Working Towards Immersion

There are three intensive learning activities that require a bit of balancing: learning from the coursebook, Anki practice, and learning directly from native-level materials. If you are unsure about how much time you can commit to language learning daily, start with doing just one of these activities for 45-90 minutes each day. Cycle between them every day and try not to get caught up in focusing on just one. They are equally important.

Whenever you're ready, try two of these intensive learning activities each day. If you can manage such a routine consistently, you will be sure to learn at an accelerated rate. Doing all three intensive learning activities every day is not recommended. When strict study time begins to exceed two or even three hours, you'll begin to run into problems similar to those mentioned in the first chapter.

After these one or two intensive learning activities are completed, you can further build upon your routine by adding in extensive activities to do in the target language. In comparison, these are much more relaxed and laid back. Think of them as hobbies to do in the foreign language. After the intensive learning sessions, take at least 20-30 minutes each day to freely read, watch, or listen to foreign material without English or interact with native speakers. Unlike the method described in the first chapter, here we aren't trying to learn anything at all. Take this time to enjoy material for the subject matter alone!

For some folks, this one to two hour commitment might be really hard to follow every day. If you are having trouble with this commitment, aim for just 45 minutes every day. Focus on not breaking the habit at all costs. Consistency builds habits.

Doing Spanish three times a week will not cut it. Languages are not just knowledge but also a set of skills our eyes, ears, mouths, hands, and heads must practice daily in order to achieve fluency. If you can only make the time to watch 20 minutes of video content with no subtitles for the day, so be it. You may not learn much for that day, but these small but consistent actions build towards new habits that will enable you to make this major lifestyle change.

If you wish to learn full-time or go full immersion in your home environment, it is highly recommended to cycle between multiple extensive activities each day in time-boxed sessions of 20-45 minutes for each activity. This includes watching fun material with no English subtitles, reading in the target language on topics that you are highly interested in, and communicating with native speakers. You can also take 20-45 minutes at a time to replace more and more of your life with the target language. Some of these steps towards immersion we can immediately get used to, but others may take years in order to overwrite old habits that are strongly rooted in our native language.

Here are some ideas. Delete all songs in English from your music library and replace it with music in Japanese or Korean. Change your computer and phone's language to French. Delete all non-essential English internet bookmarks and replace them with good German sites. And if you browse video streaming sites like YouTube often, be sure to try the Foreign Language Video Tape idea which will be discussed next chapter.

How To Master Your Textbook

Your textbook should be your loyal and faithful servant and not the other way around. Do not let it become your master. What I mean is that it should not take up the majority of your study and learning time.

Let these books briefly serve you, and then, dismiss them. Seek 5-10 minute explanations for new language and grammar structures. Don't bother with drills and grammatical exercises if they don't interest you. Don't write words out over and over. Don't bore yourself with the comprehension questions in the book. Understand the gist and get out of there! The four super flashcard exercises will make sure that we receive more than enough practice. Use your coursebook time to feed Anki the new information that you wish to practice.

Here are some general rules that may help clear some confusion on what exercises to make as you progress through your book. For new vocabulary words and set phrases, create one Production and one Listening card. For every major grammar point or topic covered, grab 3-5 sentences and make one Listening and Shadowing card. It's not necessary to turn every new sentence into an Anki card, or otherwise, you might fall asleep before you make it to the next chapter!

Create Cloze cards for new grammar points, grammar particles, and verb conjugations in these sentences. At this stage, testing new vocabulary and phrases with Cloze exercises is not recommended for the reasons stated in the last chapter. It may work, however, in larger contexts from your coursebook where it is much easier to guess the missing word. If you find a good phrase within a few sentences that you would like to master, try creating one Production card, one Listening card, one Shadowing card, and multiple Cloze cards to learn it one word at a time.

Yes, that is a lot of Cloze cards. Most textbooks will throw a large amount of vocabulary at you, so an extensive amount of Production and Listening cards will help to balance it out. This will help to keep Anki sessions fast-paced.

Declension tables can be tackled with Production and Listening exercises. These are the overwhelming tables presented in textbooks that list multiple conjugations for verbs, articles, and adjectives. For articles and adjectives, include the noun and other necessary words to test for proper use in context.

There is no need to make these cards for 100 verbs or nouns or even 10. That wouldn't be easy or fun. Try to find just a few of the most common verbs and nouns that represent the rules well and make Production and Listening cards for only the commonly used forms. Rather than make one Production and one Listening for every form, split the verbs, articles, and adjectives between the two exercises to save time. You can always make more as you learn new words.

Remember that all of these exercises should go in one deck to maximize the variety during sessions and keep you on your toes. You will never know what is coming up next. Cloze cards will make sure we learn standard phrases, conjugate verbs properly, and use the appropriate grammar particle when necessary. Production and Listening cards will provide those quick lightning round challenges to boost our recall speed and listening comprehension. Shadowing cards will work on our intonation while challenging us to keep up with the native speaker.

A Most Common Mistake

Here's where beginning language learners make the most common mistake. It's a mistake that often puts an early end to many hopeful newcomers in learning a new language. There is no need to finish your initial coursebook before you try learning directly from fun native-level materials. You don't even need to finish the book or course at all! Learn what you can from it until you get bored.

Boredom is our brain's way of telling us that we are going to burn out if we continue to push ourselves to learn from the same material day after day. Our brains are smart that way. It knows when something is no longer working. Resistance to learning doesn't mean that we are stupid or lazy. It means to stop and do something different.

It's so easy to blame ourselves for getting bored because we might feel that we should learn all this serious stuff before we get to learn from fun materials. That line of thinking, however, is not true at all. Learning from fun materials is the key to never getting bored and quitting.

Hop around materials as you personally see fit! Jump between your coursebook and your true interests in the target language. Whatever you truly desire to learn from is where you should go next. Listening to and following that desire is what keeps you learning. That's the secret to wanting to learn and improve each and every day.

If that happens to be Japanese anime or Korean pop music, so be it. Try to learn directly from native-level materials as soon as possible. When you personally make the connection between what you are learning from language learning materials to what you see in native-level materials, that will boost your motivation more than almost anything else. That is how you can eventually conquer all the serious language you feel that you should learn.

Reviewing vs Training

As you work through your first textbook, you may find that creating flashcards is much more exciting and easier than actually training with them. Watching pages turn while we advance to more topics is highly alluring, yet there must be a balance between creating and doing the exercises.

I prefer to think of Anki exercises as training rather than review. Review is something a high school or college student commonly endures to get a high grade on a upcoming test. We aren't reviewing. We are learning. If we can't recall the word or recognize it during conversation, we haven't truly learned it yet. In Anki, we are training ourselves to improve our language skill every day by recalling more and more words faster and training ourselves to understand more of the spoken and written language.

Think of these Anki sessions as training. The boxer must train his reflexes and punches to be faster than his opponent. The bodybuilder must hit his weak points as hard as he can to bring perfect balance to his body. Language learners must hit new words, phrases, and grammar points from all angles to fully develop all five of the language skills. Just knowing how to punch, how to bench press, or how to read a new word is not enough.

FOREIGN LANGUAGE VIDEO TAPE

This infant stage of language learning can become the most exciting and lively part of the whole journey. Everything is new. Our ears take in a whole range of new sounds and utterrings that we were previously unaware of.

It can also be a little uncomfortable. Learning a new language requires pushing ourselves outside of our comfort zone. Producing those new sounds and words can be a challenge. Attempts at reading are more mumbles than actual words.

We will learn so darn fast as we race forward in our first 100 days. It is somewhat like lifting weights for the first time and something called "beginner gains." It is a strange phenomenon that happens during the first few months of lifting where the body calls for the muscles to rapidly grow and potentially double in size. Our minds can undergo a similar process where the novelty and unfamiliarity of a new language allows for a massive amount of information to easily stick to our brains. Our Anki exercises will make sure that we are capitalizing on this process the entire way through.

Some folks dislike this early period because we have to learn things that aren't terribly exciting like "on, in, under, by" and "the cow says moo!" It can be humiliating especially when foreign language learning materials targeted at adults treat you otherwise. Single words are repeated three times with this awkward, unnatural pause in between. Native speakers slow down their speech to robotic levels. Textbooks contain workbook exercises that can seem like homework.

When starting from zero in Japanese, I decided that I would rather learn like a Japanese kid than an American adult. I sang "Head Shoulders Knees Toes" while standing up and touching each body part in turn. I let myself be a kid again singing simple things like "Under the Spreading Chestnut Tree." I cast aside my manly and muscly persona temporarily to "Let It Go" in Japanese. There was some slight embarrassment, but at least I was excited for the first time in a long time. So let's not be so serious.

This next technique may be worth your time if you are having trouble focusing on reading, listening to, or watching foreign material for at least 20 minutes without any English. In the beginning, our language ability is so low that it becomes really difficult to focus when we don't understand what's going on. Reading material at this stage may not be the best idea, and it may be better to stick with video and audio materials. Of course, it makes sense to try a variety of material that you are interested in, and if you are looking for something new, try this Foreign Language Video Tape technique for 20-45 minutes at a time.

So, What Is This Tape?

YouTube and other video streaming websites offer a very stimulating option to first encounter new words among other things in a new language. It also offers an activity where we can immerse ourselves in the target language. The YouTube Playlist feature and similar features on other video sharing websites allow us to build and watch a playlist of helpful and intriguing videos in the target language. Whether you are learning farm animals, greetings, or days of the week, there is a very high chance a helpful video exists in your target language.

If you limit your video searches by using English, however, you will be missing a huge opportunity. You may even find yourself watching too many videos with a native speaker repeating the word "eat" three times and only a single, stale image of a woman eating a sandwich to fixate upon. What a nightmare that would be!

If you search YouTube in the target language for a few of the words that you learned that day, I guarantee that you will find much more interesting content. What follows after we click "Search" could be described as a surge of foreign culture and society that will be of massive benefit to you. You will be surprised at the unpredictable variety of material that surfaces. Watching strings of random videos in a foreign language and trying different search terms will net you a large playlist of appealing and interesting videos.

You are likely to find a few videos aimed at preschool children, and there is nothing wrong with watching these. Let down your imaginary barriers and adult preconceptions for the sake of a new learning experience. If they make you feel overly embarrassed, you can watch them when no one is around. Cuteness and catchy Children's songs won't kill you. Some videos will be perfect for learning words like the "Head Shoulders Knees and Toes" song.

Building a Habit of Immersion

Use this Foreign Language Video Tape to build a habit of immersion early on. We are taking in and learning so much consciously and subconsciously from this prelude to the real and actual language. Don't worry if you don't understand what exactly is going on. Start with trying to understand the gist of each video. You might even be able to hear the word that you searched for.

You might have to weed through a number of dull videos to find the rare ones that offer high value to you. Think of it as receiving massive exposure to the foreign language, country, and culture. Each session you can refine your playlist and search the words that you learned that day or are related to your interests in the foreign country.

Add anything and everything interesting and remove the videos that don't have much re-watch value. Take pride in constructing a great playlist of videos that are informative, entertaining, and re-watchable. Add videos that teach you something about the country or people that you were unaware of before. Try to expand and edit your playlist each day if you are looking to take another step towards full immersion.

Re-watch the playlist as you see fit. Some language learners enjoy re-watching content multiple times in an effort to learn more and more each time. Personally, I never re-watch any content, but I use the playlist to collect cultural gems I'm really proud that I found.

Consistency is important in building a habit of freely watching, listening to, and reading material in the target language in our leisure time. Rest days away from Anki and the coursebook could certainly be a good idea, but take these days to relax in your target language. Watching and adding to your playlist could be a part of your rest day. It may even eventually lead to a new interest in the language.

PART THREE

Learn From What You Love

ESCAPE THE LANGUAGE LEARNING BUBBLE

There is no point in time where we become ready for material made by native speakers for native speakers. It is certainly not when you complete that set of six Dutch textbooks. This imaginary point in time where we will be magically ready to understand everything doesn't exist. We don't even need to understand half of everything. We just need some simple rules.

You might feel that you haven't mastered the basics after one textbook, and this feeling may definitely reflect some truth. And what about the everyday things in life in a foreign country: paying bills, renting an apartment, going to the bank, and working at a company? If you would like to live and work in the foreign country one day, a certain set of vocabulary and phrases is going to be needed. You may even wish to purchase an additional coursebook to make sure that you don't sound like another embarrassing tourist. Go for it.

This book exists to say that you will have a lot more fun and motivation in the long-term when you supplement what you learn from fun things with these language learning materials. Of course, common sense says to do things the other way around. Then again, you have so many hopeful language students who begin learning and drop out when things becomes too dry and boring.

Some folks including myself have found a series of coursebooks and textbooks to be interesting in the past because the learning process itself can be exciting. The beginning months can be highly stimulating and intriguing as we learn how to express larger and larger ideas. Some of those in the intermediate stages of a language, however, can testify to what eventually follows after the first few textbooks are completed.

You realize that you still struggle to understand most native-level material, so you buy more advanced books covering more grammar, phrases, and idioms. You go harder in your learning routine and aim to study for more than three hours per day. Grammar explanations become long and winded. And there's always more vocabulary to learn. The first few thousand came easy with a little bit of effort, but now suddenly there's 30,000 that you are expected to know!

"Fun? There's no time for that. I have to learn more", may be the last words of your motivation before it disappears. It's so easy to become trapped and confined within a bubble of language learning materials. Learning may unknowingly become stale, boring, and inefficient for months and years.

An Alternative Course

Let's use these advanced resources as references to look up any new or unfamiliar language structures when we encounter them in native-level materials. Wouldn't it be nice to quickly drop in, understand the gist of the target word or structure, and be done with these resources? Lengthy grammar explanations can easily be forgotten, yet a large context from a story that we truly care about can burn in our memory for years.

You might not even need any advanced textbook. In the age of the internet, quick searches to many questions can provide an accurate answer in just a minute or two. Online dictionaries can provide the basic meaning to an overwhelming majority of words and phrases as well as plenty of example sentences. If more explanation is desired, internet searches for target grammar structures will reveal resources that provide sufficient explanations to most structures.

As we move into native-level materials, I recommend that you keep adding to the original deck, as there will probably be a backlog of hundreds of new cards that you have created but have not been tested on yet. This information is likely to be commonly found in native-level materials, so let's keep building that strong foundation with our original deck.

When there are already 1000+ Anki cards created from coursebook material, it may take a few days to see the content mined from native-level materials show up during Anki practice. It may be tempting to start that new deck but your patience will rewarded. The new content will show up during Anki sessions if you keep your deck order mixed.

For native-level materials, we will use the same four Anki exercises: Production, Cloze, Listening, and Shadowing. In order for these exercises to be smooth and engaging, we must wisely choose our sentences from native-level materials. We will then need to learn the meaning of the new words, grammar structures, and phrases using online dictionaries, internet searches, image searches.

Without Love, All of This Learning is Meaningless

Let's switch our primary source for learning to literature, TV shows, movies, music, or whatever got us interested in the language in the first place. Let this material become our new textbook. Learning from native-level materials that you truly love to read, watch, and listen to for fun will help sustain motivation for the long-term.

Go for the heart and what you truly care about your target language and country. For Japanese learners, it is anime and manga that many people gravitate towards. Korean learners, it may be economics, politics, dramas, or even the highly competitive e-sports gaming scene. What do you truly love about the target language and country?

Foreign pop culture and TV do not have to be the end goal in learning a language. There is so much more to a language than what you might find on foreign TV. Regardless of the language and culture, low-quality TV programs can numb the mind rather than excite it. For sustaining long-term motivation for years, it's best in the long-run to find a hobby that you truly enjoy and can learn from in the target language. You will know when you find it. You will stop asking yourself the question, "is this all there is?"

Some folks may just wish to meet, befriend, and be proficient in communicating with others who speak their target language. In this case, Facebook, Twitter, and other social platforms provide instant gold mines of sentences and passages to dissect. You can bring these written words to life using AwesomeTTS and hear surprisingly somewhat natural renditions of them performed by automated speakers.

You may also find new topics to read up on through social media. Make foreign friends. Press the "Like" button on new pages. Join foreign groups that pique your interest. Follow famous people that you admire. These actions will immerse your social feed in only your target language.

If what you truly enjoy is found only in reading materials, so be it. Some of the world's most impressive polyglots claim a strong habit of extensively reading novels and literature is one of the secrets to their amazing abilities. Shadowing can be done elsewhere, and Anki does provide the Text to Speech support to place that written material in our ears at least.

It is common advice to listen to the target language daily or as often as possible for listening comprehension practice, but try asking yourself this question. Would this audio or visual material add enjoyment to my life or not? The answer is easy to figure out. If it takes more than two seconds to answer yes, it's no.

The Immersion Method

Blogs, comics, books, websites, movies, and TV programs all contain these juicy sentences to break down and learn. If you have ever tried to study any of these materials diligently in the past, however, you know how enormous a task it can be. How do we focus long enough to break down an entire online article or even a short story line by line? How do we not become overwhelmed by websites where everything is in the foreign language? How can we study a drama or an anime?

How do we keep up the willpower to continue these unsustainable study routines after just two days? The problem gets worse and worse. We burn all initial motivation pushing ourselves to break down and learn massive amounts of language until the day comes when we would rather do anything than another day of routine study.

Let's revisit the method discussed in the first chapter but this time go into more detail. Immerse yourself in the foreign material that you love without any English assistance for roughly 20 minutes. As you carefully read, watch, and listen, identify the words unknown to you and that are repeated multiple times. Quickly write down the unknown words that are repeated two or more times and continue without looking anything up in the dictionary nor stopping the reading, video, or audio. Include the page numbers, video times, audio track times, and screenshots for reference later.

After the 20 minutes or so have passed, you will need to pick just two small passages that you are highly interested in learning. In the case of audio and video materials, you will need transcriptions. For the purposes of this book, one passage can be a single long sentence, a few sentences, or even brief dialogues (two to three lines).

There is no need to translate entire short stories or drama episodes when looking for these sentences and passages. This is why it's important to train the immersion habit from the very beginning, so we are comfortable and secure not understanding everything. We don't want to burn ourselves out from over-extending our desire to learn too quickly. A few sentences each day along with fun, immersion, and consistency are key.

There is an amazing process that slowly blooms as you read, watch, and mine a single topic for sentences. When you mine passages over and over from a particular subject matter for weeks and months, you will come to know its most commonly used words and phrases. Once you have a strong grasp on the high frequency words, you will be able to piece together more and more of the meaning of new content from that source as you first hear or see it.

When new words and sentences come from a much larger story or plot that you are highly interested in, all that new information becomes so much more memorable. Almost every line has character to it, and they can become unforgettable. It's the power of context.

Forget the Rest!

Listen, watch, or read as you normally do in English. Watch videos and read materials once or twice and no more. Don't watch the same video, movie, or TV episode over and over until you break down everything from it for the sake of learning. I am guilty of doing this myself in the past, and to cite personal experience, it will cause agony and madness to slowly creep in. Learning just a few lines of dialogue from each episode or chapter is enough to move on to the next one.

That last line is so vital to making all of this learning fun, so I would like to repeat it. Learning just a few words or lines of dialogue from each episode or chapter is enough to move on to the next one.

But why two passages and not three passages? Each passage does require a significant amount of work. The process of breaking down and learning the sentences, looking up new words and grammar points, searching for answers to potential questions we might have, and creating the Anki cards takes a good chunk of time. Two can take from anywhere from 45 minutes to two hours (including the immersion time) depending on how curious you are and the speed you work at. For the sake of consistency, I recommend two, but three is definitely possible. Four raises a lot of doubts in mind.

Native Speakers Do Not Talk Too Fast

Using English subtitles to watch foreign TV shows, movies, dramas, and videos is an English reading activity with some background noise. You will learn nothing outside a few basic words. You might be tempted to use them to help you focus on the story or relax after an intense study session, but if you choose to use them, native speakers will always talk too fast for you.

They will always talk too fast unless you take the time each and every day to practice trying to comprehend what they mean. But how can we comprehend them in the beginner and intermediate stages when they use thousands of words that we do not know yet? Listening comprehension is a skill that is built through practicing with whatever vocabulary that we do know at the time and relying on context for the words that we do not know.

We will understand the foreign language only by consistently trying to understand the foreign language. Anki exercises are amazingly helpful, but we need every chance that we can get to build towards our reading and listening abilities. Some people like to cite that it takes roughly 10,000 hours of practice to achieve a high level of skill in anything, and this number may or may not be completely accurate. The value of consistent practice, however, is something most of us can agree on.

Listening comprehension is arguably the weakest skill of the average language learner, for most instruction of the target language is provided through text or explanations in the learner's native tongue. While audio tracks accompanying language courses are certainly helpful, you may quickly find that they do not provide the volume of practice necessary to understand native speakers out in the everyday world.

While subtitles in the target language are extremely helpful to learning key moments from video materials, it's poison to our listening comprehension ability. Sadly, these subtitles don't come equipped with the native speakers that you encounter in the real world. So, let's turn these subtitles off, too. They are a reading exercise, which is definitely an improvement over an English one, but we will get plenty of that later in our Anki exercises and while freely reading native-level material.

We don't have a foreign mommy and daddy to speak to us every day for 8-12 hours for 10+ years. You can pay tutors to do just that, but that becomes expensive to do every day for even one hour a day. Without these adult native speakers constantly around, our ears remain incredibly weak. We have a lot of catching up to do. Listening to native-level materials every day and the Listening exercises in this book's method will help to alleviate this problem.

If you would like to learn from music, song lyrics would be an exception to this rule. Singing the correct lyrics is already a difficult endeavor in our native language, and mishearing lyrics is just as common as it is funny. Start with the lyrics and make it a game to work your way towards relying less and less on them. If you don't want to sing and would rather just listen, this won't do at all. You are missing a huge opportunity to improve your pronunciation, learn language through mimicry, and have quite a lot of fun.

No Subtitles, But How?

If there are irremovable English subtitles in a video, we can block them from view by cutting out and placing a wide but short piece of thick paper in front of our computer screens. We will not need the subtitles and transcripts until we have found our passages for learning, but until then, train your ears to find the words that are both unknown to you and that are repeated frequently. The moments we desire to understand the most can also become one of our passages for the day. Simply jot down the video time for later reference and don't press pause.

Consistently consuming foreign material and watching the Foreign Language Video Tape up to this point will be of major help, yet when English translations suddenly become available, it can be fairly difficult to keep them out for some folks. You will be tested. You will need determination and faith to fight against the habit of doing everything in English. If allowed even for a brief moment, we feed ourselves the idea that we must understand everything to get the most enjoyment from the material. This idea, however, is a lie that we tell ourselves.

Watch and read things where the premise is easily understandable. It would be a great idea to re-watch favorite TV shows and movies that you originally saw in English but now dubbed in the target language. Despite how good it may be for listening practice, it can be maddening watching the same episode or movie five or more times, so I recommend watching and reading how we normally would in our native language. Once or twice is sufficient.

Work towards building and maintaining a habit of freely reading, listening, and watching without stopping. Do not continually stop to look up words and phrases. Do not look up anything at all until the brief immersion period ends. Trying new material and getting lost quickly is frustrating, but when we do possess something that we personally find exciting and can understand the gist, it's enough. When we finally realize that we do not need to understand everything said and can still enjoy our favorite material, we have won!

Choose Easy

At the end of the immersion time, you'll have a list of words, video times, and page numbers to review, but some of these potential passages could be too difficult for your current level. If you select contexts with four or more unknown words altogether, it's still possible to break down all the vocabulary and grammatical information. Yet so many new words, phrases, and grammar points can raise numerous questions to look up and make the learning process slow-paced and painful.

Repeatedly choosing these types of passages can lead to frustrating Cloze and Shadowing exercises. Shadowing becomes a nuisance when there are too many new words and too much unfamiliar language. Our tongues will seemingly freeze up when the difficulty bar is set too high. During a Cloze exercise, we won't be able to figure out the missing word if there are too many unknown words in the context. These kinds of exercises will cause boredom and make Anki very tedious.

Choosing easy can make learning so much more fun and even addictive. Choosing contexts with just one, two, or three new words allows learning to happen seemingly at a faster pace. When the level of the challenge before us is just at the perfect level, we can enter a flow-like state where our learning becomes much more pleasurable and satisfying.

Double Check Your Work

Hunting and obtaining the subtitles and transcripts for specific audio and video materials can be a challenge, and the level of difficulty varies for every language. Yet once they are in our hands, learning straight from the material that you love becomes possible. For instance, we can use the free website http://kitsunekko.net to find Japanese subtitles for almost any anime out there. And for Korean, Viki (https://www.viki.com) offers Korean subtitles for some of the more popular K-Dramas.

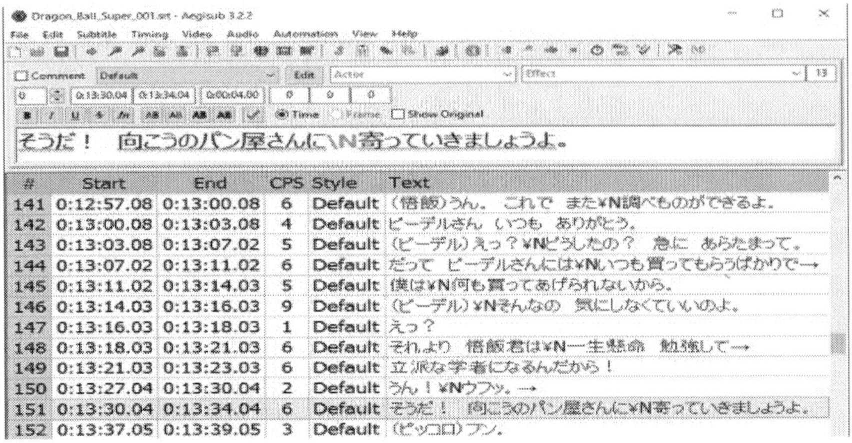
Dragon_Ball_Super_001.srt - Aegisub 3.2.2
File Edit Subtitle Timing Video Audio Automation View Help
Comment
Default
Edit
Actor
Effect
Time
Frame
Show Original
そうだ！　向こうのパン屋さんに\N寄っていきましょうよ。
Start End CPS Style Text
141 0:12:57.08 0:13:00.08 6 Default （悟飯）うん。 これで また¥N調べものができるよ。
142 0:13:00.08 0:13:03.08 4 Default ビーデルさん いつも ありがとう。
143 0:13:03.08 0:13:07.02 5 Default （ビーデル）えっ？¥Nどうしたの？ 急に あらたまって。
144 0:13:07.02 0:13:11.02 6 Default だって ビーデルさんには¥Nいつも買ってもらうばかりで→
145 0:13:11.02 0:13:14.03 5 Default 僕は¥N何も買ってあげられないから。
146 0:13:14.03 0:13:16.03 9 Default （ビーデル）¥Nそんなの 気にしなくていいのよ。
147 0:13:16.03 0:13:18.03 1 Default えっ？
148 0:13:18.03 0:13:21.03 6 Default それより 悟飯君は¥N一生懸命 勉強して→
149 0:13:21.03 0:13:23.03 6 Default 立派な学者になるんだから！
150 0:13:27.04 0:13:30.04 2 Default うん！¥Nウフッ。→
151 0:13:30.04 0:13:34.04 6 Default そうだ！ 向こうのパン屋さんに¥N寄っていきましょうよ。
152 0:13:37.05 0:13:39.05 3 Default （ピッコロ）フン。

JAPANESE SUBTITLES FOR DRAGON BALL SUPER EPISODE 1

Once we have broken down the new passages and learned the new words and grammatical information, we will have a far better understanding of their meaning. Understanding the exact meaning behind the words can be tricky from time to time. It can be very easy to miss the underlying tone and hidden connotation in foreign languages, and this becomes more apparent whenever language is translated. Perhaps you have seen the results of this on photos of funny T-shirts or inappropriately translated signs in Asia. We wouldn't want the same thing to happen to us when we spoke or wrote something, right?

We should use the English subtitles to double check the meaning that we came up with in our head. Don't use English subtitles and translations when freely watching and reading foreign material. After our 20 minutes or so has ended and the passages for learning have been selected, it is OK to check the English subtitles to clarify any underlying tone and meaning in the words. It is highly important to make sure that we completely understand what we are trying to learn before we put it into practice. Language textbooks usually provide English translations for this reason.

All this subtitle and translation talk might sound somewhat contradictory, so here's an easier way to think about it. Native-level materials are for long and extensive listening and reading practice. Subtitles and translations are for short and intensive learning.

SUPER ANKI

We will see the same sentences frequently during our first few Anki sessions, but soon a large variety of hundreds of sentences will take form. Within a few weeks, we will amass a diverse bank of sentences to practice from, and we will rarely see the same passage more than once or twice in a session. Seeing this massive range of words and contexts through the four Anki exercises will do many things for us:

1. Allow us to visit a variety of topics in rapid succession.
2. Test our ability to recall words through reading, writing, speaking, and listening.
3. Keep us on our toes with the uncertainty of what is to come next.
4. Enable learning to flow like a fast-paced game.

Cloze Upgrades

Cloze cards will receive a significant upgrade. After moving on to native-level materials, we will be ready for longer and more memorable contexts which will allow us to test for vocabulary and set phrases rather than just grammar and verb conjugations.

It's still recommended, however, to test only one word at a time. Learn new expressions one word at a time. Test new language structures one word at a time. Make cards for even the easy vocabulary you are very familiar with that are found within new structures and phrases. It's an easy way to learn. We will strengthen our reading, thinking, and writing skills and build our vocabulary up with virtually no stress.

Imagine that we wanted to learn a new expression or phrase composed of a group of words, and we created a single Cloze card where we needed to write this group of words. When several words are missing and there is less context to work with, multiple possible answers can come to mind. We would have to remember the exact group of words missing in the sentence from all the possible synonyms.

If you're learning to write Chinese hanzi or Japanese kanji with Cloze cards, test one hanzi or kanji character at a time rather than single words that may contain one, two, or three or more characters within it. It's much easier and efficient to practice recalling the writing of just one character and know its one meaning and one reading in that context. If you test for two or more of these highly complex characters at a time, problems from lack of clear context can begin to accumulate.

Inserting Images and Audio

Images and audio aren't required, but they are a means to create a stronger link to what we are learning inside Anki to what we are watching and listening to every day. Images and the original audio files can make Anki all the more real, and your efforts here will be rewarded.

Images and audio from videos can be useful in Cloze and Shadowing cards to add context. They are super easy to insert. Press the 'PrtSc' button (Command + Shift + 3 for Macs) on your keyboard while the video is on the screen and paused at the appropriate moment. Then, we will need to open up a basic image editing program like Paint in Windows (Paintbrush for Macs) and crop the image to our liking before saving it. When adding Cloze and Shadowing cards to Anki, make sure the cursor is in the 'Front' text box, and click the paperclip icon to add our image.

Inserting audio is a little more difficult. For educational purposes, you will need to download the original audio, extract video files from the CD or DVD you have purchased, or find the files elsewhere legally. There are of course many ways to create the audio clip we want, but I found the free audio editing program Audacity (http://www.audacityteam.org) to work well enough.

In order to import video files into Audacity, however, we will need to install the FFmpeg library file. This add-on is supported by the Audacity developers and is provided on their website. It can also be found with a simple internet search with the words "FFmpeg library audacity."

FFmpeg Library for Audacity:

http://manual.audacityteam.org/man/faq_installation_and_plug_ins.html#How_do_I_download_and_install_the_FFmpeg_Import.2FExport_Library.3F

After opening the file with Audacity, we can use the times in the original audio or video file to find our selected passage with ease. Use the mouse to highlight the clip needed, press the stop button, and go to 'File' and then 'Export Selected Audio...' to create the audio clip needed. We can use the paperclip icon in Anki to insert these audio clips in Cloze and Shadowing exercises just as we did with the images.

I have found the audio clip from our anime example last chapter:

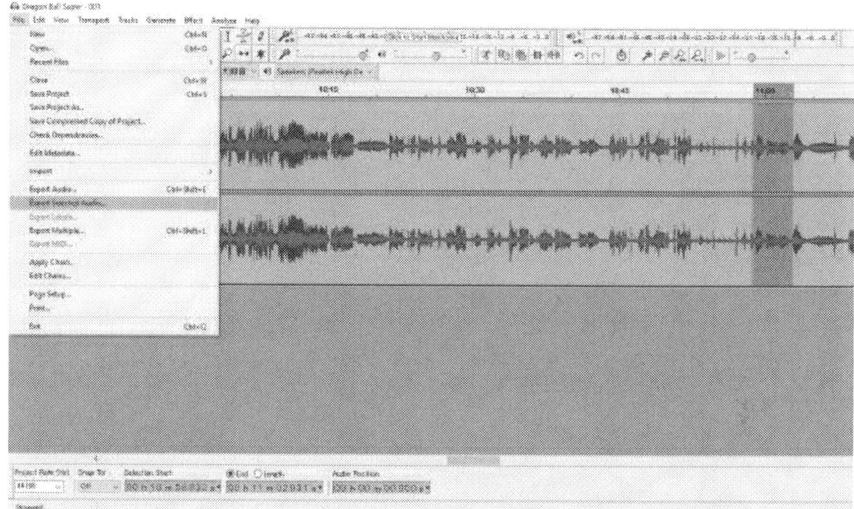

EXTRACTING AUDIO FROM VIDEO WITH AUDACITY

How To Learn Vocabulary Really Fast

Ultimately, you may use the Anki exercises any way that you wish, but here is how I would dissect new passages. New words and phrases get one Production and one Listening card, and Cloze cards can be used if you think there is enough context. New or unfamiliar grammar structures get one Cloze card. For Shadowing, make two or three duplicate cards to help balance out the ratio. Create one Listening card for the entire passage, but that is just the start.

For Listening cards, here is where we can take it to the next level and learn hundreds of words with relative ease. Use online dictionaries to find one or two sample sentences for each of the new words and phrases from the passage. Create Listening cards for these one or two sample sentences. If they contain the new word or phrase plus two or three new words, it will be too difficult. If they contain just one additional new word, however, that is perfect! Take this additional new word from the sample sentence and create one Production and one Listening card.

You can repeat this cycle by finding new sample sentences for these new words! Continue for however long you like. In the end, you will create a ton of Listening cards, and this makes for very simple and fast Anki sessions considering they are the easiest exercise. They are my personal favorite way to use Anki, but you might be happier with a different ratio of cards.

If we learned the phrase "do in advance" from our chosen passage for instance, we can do some work and attack it from several diverse angles. Here are five sample phrases that we might find in the dictionary or in our grammar book: "do homework in advance", "do prep work in advance", "be ready in advance", "tell her in advance", and "pay rent in advance".

Example Passage

For this example, I will use a Japanese sentence written in its most basic alphabet with none of the complex kanji characters. This is to model how Cloze exercises can be done akin to most other foreign languages. Here's just one way you could make Anki exercises for this sentence.

Sample Passage:

かのじょはとくべつなつくりかたでぱんをやいている。

She has a special way of making (baking) bread.

special

PRODUCTION # 1: **とくべつ**

(the act of) making

PRODUCTION # 2: つくり

way (of doing something)

***PRODUCTION # 3:* かた**

(It's) baking

PRODUCTION # 4: やいている

かのじょはとくべつ[...]つくり

かたでぱんをやいている。

CLOZE # 1: な, GRAMMATICAL RULE WITH JAPANESE ADJECTIVES

かのじょはとくべつなつくり

かた [...] ぱんをやいている。

CLOZE # 2: で, "OF", GRAMMAR PARTICLE

かのじょはとくべつなつくり

[...]でぱんをやいている。

CLOZE # 3: かた, *"WAY"*

かのじょはとくべつな

つくりかたでぱんを[...]。

CLOZE # 4:* やいている*, "BAKING", TESTING FOR VERB CONJUGATION

とくべつ

(Audio file)

LISTENING # 1: SPECIAL

つくり

(Audio file)

LISTENING # 2: (THE ACT OF) MAKING

かた

(Audio file)

LISTENING # 3: WAY (OF DOING SOMETHING)

やいている

(Audio file)

LISTENING # 4: (IT'S) BAKING

とくべつなとびかた

(Audio file)

LISTENING # 5: SPECIAL WAY OF JUMPING

とくべつななげかた

(Audio file)

LISTENING # 6: SPECIAL WAY OF THROWING

天ぷらの作り方を本で読みました。

(Audio file)

LISTENING # 7: I READ ABOUT HOW TO MAKE TEMPURA IN A BOOK.

彼は模型飛行機作りに夢中だ。

(Audio file)

LISTENING # 8: HE IS INTO MAKING MODEL AIRPLANES.

かのじょはとくべつなつくり

かたでぱんをやいている。

SHADOWING # 1

かのじょはとくべつなつくり

かたでぱんをやいている。。

SHADOWING # 2

かのじょはとくべつなつくり

かたでぱんをやいている。。。

SHADOWING # 3

CONSISTENCY, ROUTINE, AND HABIT

I remember growing up disliking the word 'schedule' and the idea of scheduling things. It seemed like something for uptight and OCD people who do things in an overly controlled manner. I had this impression that if I started scheduling things, I would start to create these over-the-top schedules in which every last minute contained something to do. There would be no time for any fun!

When it comes to taking action towards creating new habits, however, there is a universal truth that we must face. If it does not get scheduled, it does not get done. We must decide on —and then commit to —a routine that we will follow every day, as faithfully as we can. There must be a very specific time during the day when we will do our passage mining, learning, and Anki training. Otherwise, lesser tasks and distractions sneak in, and the age-old excuse of "I couldn't find the time..." starts coming out of our mouths. That classic excuse signals that we never took the next step to set up a specific time and place.

Go ahead and set a specific time of day when you have 45 to 90 minutes to start on the following routine. Once again, I recommend the early morning before work or school or right afterward to make it the most important priority while we still have the momentum to get things done.

Sample Starting Schedule:

Monday - Two new passages

Tuesday - Two new passages

Wednesday - Two new passages

Thursday - Anki 10 new cards / 10 due cards

Friday - Anki 10 new cards / 10 due cards

Saturday —Anki 10 new cards / 10 due cards

Sunday —Extensive listening / reading

I encourage you to play around with this starting schedule and make it your own. This is just merely a template for you to start with and improve on. Test your own ideas and see what brings the most learning and enjoyment to your own program.

Some language learners believe in speaking and interacting with native speakers each and every day starting even from day one. That may require a completely different schedule than what I have provided.

Our brains can be sapped after 45-90 minutes of intensive learning and Anki training, but it is important to take at least an additional 20-30 minutes each day to read, listen to, and watch material in the target language to keep up the immersion habit. We need to train our ears and eyes daily if we desire to hit high levels of proficiency and fluency.

If you are looking to speed up the learning process, try learning two passages and doing the Anki sessions on the same day. Now, this might take you a little over two hours, so maintaining this level of commitment is only recommended for those feeling extra motivated. Make sure to take some sort of break between these two intensive learning activities. You could do three passages or longer Anki sessions, but switching between these two different activities is recommended to maximize your attention span and enjoyment.

If you are looking to learn full-time or even go full immersion in your home environment, it would be wise to keep our daily passage learning and Anki sessions under three hours. There comes a point in time while learning where you might find it much more productive to allocate your time to multiple activities rather than more study. Activities such as the Foreign Language Video Tape, interacting with native speakers, or freely watching and reading native-level materials with no English can be done as frequently as you like, as they do not require as much focus as intensive learning does.

You may even need to take one or two days off from Anki occasionally and do things in the target language for enjoyment alone. Sing songs. Play some video games. Read up on topics that interest you. Watch videos, dramas, and movies with no subtitles. Binge watching is highly encouraged!

Lang-8, Italki, and HelloTalk

Shadowing helps our speech patterns to sound more native-like while working to reduce our accent, yet we need to practice communicating our own thoughts and make sure other people can comprehend them. While living, working, and learning Korean in South Korea years ago, I felt great finally being able to continually talk in Korean with friends for hours, yet being understood all the time was another issue. Sometimes, we will string together words and grammar that make perfect sense in our head, yet we will be shocked when the listening party tells us that they have no idea what we just said.

Lang-8 (http://lang-8.com) is a free language exchange website where users make posts in the language that they wish to practice. You receive corrections in exchange for correcting other people's posts in your native language. Users can write about anything. We can write about what has been on our minds all day or even specific topics that we are interested in. When we correct other people's posts, corrections for our entries come within hours.

Personally, I found Lang-8 to be the most effective in terms of time and money. It is very convenient to visit the page at any time, write for 10-20 minutes, and leave to go about our day. Later during the same day, we can return to find the corrections and make sure we never forget them. How? Create Anki exercises.

If you are willing to pay a few dollars a session to speak with tutors face to face, Italki (https://www.italki.com) may be the better alternative. You will need to search for a teacher of your liking, schedule for an available time slot, and be logged on the video-calling software Skype (https://www.skype.com) at that time. Good teachers will send you notes of their corrections, so you will still be able to create Anki exercises from what you have learned. Face-to-face conversation and tutoring does have its advantages, so the decision to use Lang-8 or Italki or both will be left to you.

HelloTalk (https://www.hellotalk.com) is a highly popular app that has opened new possibilities of language exchange through texting. Most language learners rate this app very positively, as it possibly the most convenient way to connect directly with native speakers of almost any language that you are interested in learning. It is a great platform to start organic conversations with other users while you make new friends and correct each other as you both progress. Texting certainly takes the pressure off of face to face conversations in meeting new people through new languages, so this may be the choice for you.

Start With 10/10 Sessions

I would like to clarify some terms to make the follow discussion easier to understand. Anki practice sessions entails doing new cards (color coded blue in Anki) and review cards (color coded green in Anki under "Due"). New cards are cards that we have created but not yet seen during practice sessions. Review cards have been viewed at least once before. So, 10/10 refers to doing an Anki session with 10 new cards and 10 review cards.

The last order of business is set the order of the reviews and change the number of cards per session to 10 new cards and 10 review cards. This can easily be done by opening Anki, clicking on the gear to the right of your deck, and selecting 'Options'. Set 'New cards/day' to 10, and then click the 'Reviews' tab and set 'Maximum reviews/day' to 10. The cards are reviewed in the order that they are made by default, so to make sure we see a nice medley of different words, phrases, and sentences, shuffling the cards is recommended and also easy to do. In do so, click the 'New cards' tab, look for 'Order', and select 'Show new cards in random order'. These settings should be good enough to start with.

100 "Maximum reviews/day" is the current default setting in Anki at the time of writing this book, but if we keep this setting and complete the entire review every day, Anki practice sessions alone will quickly start exceeding 90 minutes daily. This does not include the time it takes to learn new material and create cards for them.

Why not be a diligent student and and do all the review cards no matter what it takes? Language learning is not a test. It is a hobby to do in our free time. It should be fun! Exercising, lifting weights, and playing intense sports all have some pain and fatigue involved but also a considerably large amount of endorphins (the 'feel good' chemical) that we can receive in return. Foreign language learning is the same. We must cap pain and fatigue and maximize enjoyment on a daily basis to create a long-term language learning habit.

The starting recommendation is set at 10/10 cards during Anki practice sessions, and a high amount of caution is advised if you would like to increase those numbers. Put on some safety gloves before touching this dangerous electrical current that can easily shock all the motivation out of you. Dividing Anki sessions into small time blocks throughout the day is a wise idea if you are thinking about doing more Anki.

Doing 50+ cards each day can be highly detrimental to our success. More Anki does not mean more learning and progress if it causes your internal fun and motivation meter to plummet and approach zero. During my days in Korea, I was obsessed with disciplining myself to do more than two hours of Anki per day and trying to cram in more and more Anki cards throughout my day. There was a little pleasure but so much pain and misery. I also stopped doing them for weeks at a time. Let's stop training for the Agony Olympics and hellish ultra-marathons of needlessly long Anki sessions. You will do exponentially more Anki cards just by doing it consistently as a habit.

Even when we hit our personal goals, we will not run out of new things to learn and practice. Consistency with Anki is what will keep us learning until that point and even past it while we aim at higher goals. After a certain amount of time (45-60 minutes for me personally), Anki gets boring even with a good mix of exercises. Stop right before you get bored and keep yourself hungry for the next session.

Experiment with your routine. You could do 5/5 cards every day and still have time to create new cards from new material. If you want to incorporate more Anki practice, a large number such as 25/25 could potentially be done if broken into two or more different sessions throughout the day. Most folks work tiring full-time positions like myself, so doing 10/10 sessions might lead to more consistent results.

Start with 5/5 reviews if you have trouble focusing during 10/10 reviews. Train to grow stronger in both the language ability and your ability to focus deeply. A habit of waking up and going straight to social media is highly detrimental to our ability to deeply focus. Start your day with morning walks and inspirational audiobooks to draw your focus away from everything happening around you so that you can focus on everything happening within you.

If for whatever reason you no longer like a card or sentence that you learned weeks or months ago, it's time to delete that sucker. Don't continue to learn from material that you do not enjoy and that causes you to lose motivation. This has happened to me for not just a handful of cards. I have forgotten entire decks on multiple devices. I am sure that you will undergo a similar process of creation and destruction. Do not be discouraged. In fact, we should embrace it as part of the learning process and the learning-about-learning process.

The End

Thank you so much for taking the time to read my book! If you have renewed hope for foreign language study, at least a little, please take a minute to review the book now on Amazon if you have not already. Tell me what you liked and disliked, and your suggestions might make it into the next edition.

If you would like more information, explanations, and examples, come visit my YouTube channel Fluent Japanese From Anime. There are some videos specifically made for Japanese, but you will find plenty of content that is aimed towards all language learners.

(www.youtube.com/c/FluentJapaneseFromAnime)

Made in the USA
Columbia, SC
08 March 2019